What Girls Do in the Dark

What Girls Do in the Dark

Rosie Garland

Nine
Arches
Press

What Girls Do in the Dark
Rosie Garland

ISBN: 978-1-913437-05-3
eISBN: 978-1-913437-06-0

First published October 2020 by:

Nine Arches Press
Unit 14, Sir Frank Whittle Business Centre,
Great Central Way, Rugby.
CV21 3XH
United Kingdom

www.ninearchespress.com

Nine Arches Press is supported using public funding by Arts Council England.

On December 10th 2018, the Voyager 2 explorer spacecraft left this solar system, and so did my father. To infinity and beyond.

Contents

Letter of rejection from a Black Hole

We're touched by your desire to join our great work
of dismembering the fabric of time and matter.
We can't blame you for wanting to hide in nothing,
and note the ways you've snapped off pieces of yourself
to prove you're serious.

However, we wonder if you've misunderstood our purpose;
the difference between obliteration of the cosmos and the spirit.
You've been smothering your radiance for so long
it's become a system of belief

that you're cored with lead, incapable of anything
but borrowed light, or – in a destructive twist of logic
that impressed the selection panel –
brilliance is only permitted to serve others' needs.

You have the right to glow.
It's not your duty
to light up anyone else's day.
We urge you to reconsider, wish you well,
and suggest steering clear of holes.

Trans-Neptunian objects

Way out there, between matter and not-quite void,
they weave in rocky gangs. Rag-tag remnants

of the solar system's sober gathering, they crash
each other's parties, spit geysers of methane ice,

break the law of what is and isn't planet.
They will not kneel in perfect circles round the sun,

won't toe any ordered line. There's nowt so queer
as Pluto, Sedne, Eris, Thule, Makemake.

Shoved too far for any naked eye, it only looks
like lonely. Faces cratered with a million kisses,

their drunken stagger round the Kuiper Belt
so leisurely we have galloped from cave to red button

before they've notched a handful of orbits. They squint
at our blur. We are grit in their eye. Blink and we're long gone.

Snuffing hearts that burn too bright

Just my luck. One seat left on the bus, next to a star. I jab it with my elbow, in case it gets any clever ideas and tries to spill over onto my half. It shrinks against the window, which buckles, glassy tears pooling along the black rubber seal. The star blushes, embarrassed combustion tickling the baby on the row behind. The child gurgles, grabbing for plumes of feathered stuff and nonsense. If I were its mother, I'd be on my feet, banging on the driver's window. Some people don't know the meaning of stranger danger. I smell singed wool. The star peers at me, anxious, shaking its head when I accuse it of scorching my coat. It'll deny everything. I've read how stars live off lies. So what about their surface temperature, cores of liquid helium spinning at a thousand miles per second, how they live for billions of years; haven't they got enough space in the sky to show off how glorious they are? And the eyes. One look and bang, you're gone. Not me. I know how to deal with heavenly bodies. Stars aren't the only ones who can burn things to a crisp. I could parch the sea to sand if I put my mind to it. I've binned fairy lights the day after Christmas, set out full buckets on Bonfire Night. Diaries, letters, cards, endless boring children's drawings, all tossed out with the ash. At my stop, I give my sleeve a good shake, trail diamond confetti onto the pavement. There it is, face pressed to the window, hoping I'll look back.

Yorkshire lights

The *aurora borealis* may be seen as far south as Yorkshire,
although the display is dull and brownish in colour.
– *Encyclopaedia Britannica*

You think it's a trick of the clouds, but this is no will o' the wisp
that shimmers into nothing; no sleight of hand sleek flicker

that plucks a penny from your ear while it picks your pocket.
These are slow lights, sure lights; built for the long haul. Banked fires

of bronze peat to outlast winter, rusty with the mucked-up
brass of shuttered shops, stoppered coalmines, empty wallets.
A flag steeped in bloody-mindedness. The opposite of surrender.

Steady as the rain that grinds the Pennines. True as the Leeds
        and Liverpool Canal
with its deep cut through moors marked out with sheep, daubed red.

It takes less time than you think to adjust glare-adapted eyes,
relearn the lessons of iron light. Reclaim night vision.

Making Thunder Roar

She curls her hair, eavesdrops the crackling singe.
The tongs hiss, whisper joys and horrors:
beloved ghosts that redden the horizon,
windows bursting with prisoned fire.

She pricks herself into stocking tops:
one letter, two. In darkness they multiply;
unlock their stitches, unravel into words
that itch against the soft flesh of her thigh.

She blazes story. Shimmers the room
like the waver of air above a seething pot.
Can't square this furnace passion
with the dregs that rattle in her breast.

With the dip of a nib, she is far away. Fingers tipped
with ink, she carries boundless worlds
in every striding step. Stokes heat to battle
the moor's damp wheeze. Blooms beneath broad skies.

Palimpsest

Adopted at seven months, I grow quick
into my new family's name, all flowers and gardens,
and me with thumbs that wilt roses.

I skin knees, scab knuckles, grime fingernails
and raise eyebrows with *where*
does she get it from? Good at stories, I fail

biology. Alone in my class I lack the knack
of mirroring a father's nose, a mother's chin; can't figure how
to plagiarise their features into my own.

Three decades later, I fight for my certificate; a history
kept secret from its rightful owner. It lists a stranger
mother, blank box father, my self unrecognisable, spelled all wrong.

Only the date's correct. Birthed on a Sunday,
but there's nothing bonny in Blight, nor good, nor gay.
Whichever way I twist it – Bly, Blythe – the root is rotten.

I have a pair of parent names to choose from:
half Sunday lucky, half Wednesday woeful, neither
the whole picture. A contradiction

of bloom and blotch, sickness and growth.
One for each hand to reach up and grasp,
sing 1-2-3 and swing.

Caroline Herschel observes the conjunction of Jupiter and Saturn, June 1783

It is an *o*, captured in a larger *O*.
Blush of scarlet in the lower hemisphere
where a mouth would be.

He drizzles gravy down his shirt, a constellation
of dim brown stars that take an afternoon of lye
to whiten. The hours it takes to grind glass
to precise curvature; to polish mirrors.

Eye to the spyhole. A flock of shepherd moons
herd ice into rings of such perfection
they could wed the heavens.

A smear of grease on the lens:
she calculates the shape of lips
kissing a distant lover.

What girls do in the dark

My sister goes missing for nights at a time. She's always home by the time Mum bangs on the door and yells at us to get out of bed, so there's no point in telling. Not that I would. I set my phone to wake me at 5am. Her bed's still empty. I almost fall asleep again, but at half past she comes through the window, gathering her legs beneath her in a crouch and flattening her ears. *Mum'll never believe you*, she purrs, reeling in her tail. She takes a deep breath and turns her skin the other way, so hair is on the inside and girl is on the outside. *Show me*, I say. Her eyes glimmer.

When   *you're*   *ready.*

But!

I didn't say never. You'll be good at it. Soon. But first, stop asking.

Heirlooms

Grandmother thumbs the knotted skin above her right eye,
where they removed her horn. It was a long time ago, she says.
Back when they wouldn't let folk like us keep them.
It will be different for you. Don't let anyone prune away
the strangeness that makes you strong. When I ask about Ma,
she smiles, says these things skip a generation.

She unbuttons her blouse. The scar where her left breast used to be
is wide enough to post a letter. I lost my heart to love,
she says, drawing a fingertip along the puckered skin.
She describes the crimson pearl of it, shucked from the oyster shell
of her ribs, still quivering. Did you cry? I ask. Of course, she says.
A woman must cry, to wash away the poison of discontent.

She lifts her skirt, shows the crescent stitching
from hip-bone to thigh. From this I birthed my twin,
she says. To her I give my aches and pains; my injuries.
She stores them safe, away from harm.
One day you will discover your own twin
to walk alongside you through life's bombardment.

Grandmother sings me to sleep. Her stories are true
on the inside, where it matters.
The outside is embroidery. I dream of knives
pricking their needlepoint into my flesh.
She comes into my dream and whispers:
don't wish for wounds too soon.

How can a woman sleep when the Master is in pain?

In her room beneath the eaves, she listens.
Laughter twists up the screw of the back stairs.
The Master struggles to be heard
above his wife's shrill squeal. She knows how men are trapped
in marriages; how women entice and steal what is not theirs.

Her cheek beats a heavy pulse against Master's
bedroom door. She stretches the small hours
with the pricking of her blood into Master's shirt cuffs;
unpicks the seams of Mistress's gowns, sews them
a shade tighter. Slides a curtain ring along her finger.

The Mistress writes. *It is poetry*, says Mistress,
although no question was asked. She heats the tongs,
curls Mistress's hair, peers at the dapple of ink on paper.
She does not need the skill of letters to know
the telltale shape of lies about the Master.

All that twittering of the quill, when all a woman needs to do
is spread her arms and cry, *God. Yes.* She will show him.
She will mend his jailored heart. Will keep her eyes down
and never laugh unless he draws it from her
as a man persuades a shy beast to his outstretched hand.

When Master is away, for men must go
in order to return, the house-bones creak. At night,
she sifts sugar into the ruts between the boards,
loosens stair-rods, rubs the banisters with buttered paper,
peels back the rug and polishes the floor.

The half-hour before dawn finds her sharpening knives.
She breakfasts on oats and water;
doesn't hold with honey, milk,
things that distract the tongue's attention.
On the driveway beneath the yews, the crackle of rooks.

Eloping with a comet

Breathless with forbidden flight, I grasp his tail,
hang on. Drunk on escape velocity, I boot night in the ribs,
ride the sky till it runs out of *I told you so's*.
Made it, Ma. Top of the world.

He drags me out of signal range of family, friends,
so fast it rips breath from lungs, trousseau from my fist.
Won't need either where we're headed. Shut off
the warnings of burnt fingers, snapped heart.

Doesn't everyone win some, lose some
in love's true adventure? Those first dates!
Snatched midnights, a dash home before sunrise.
Prince-shaped hero, the size of dreams come true,

he picks me out of millions. Life from dull
to dazzling at the flick of his switch. Why walk,
when I can kick home from my heels, grow fat
on promises of fly me to the moon? It's a hoot,

a whoop, a loop-de-loop as we crack
the furnace edge of atmosphere that sears
my skin to shrapnel. Cells stream in a bridal train
of blood and bone. Too cold to count the zeros

that make up absolute. I learn love the harsh way:
hitch my wagon to a rock; mistake lustre for love.
There are no battleships off the shoulder of Orion. No
C-Beams glittering off the Tannhäuser Gate.

The topiary garden

She spreads the petals of her skirt, the dress of a child
two decades past its wear-by date. She kneels, peers

into the pond's looking-glass. The water flusters
with fish, tiny as eyelashes striped with mascara.

She eases one foot from its shoe. Sticking-plaster unpeels,
heel wet with a blister's weeping.

On the first day she spent all her money:
Hello Kitty hairgrips, a matching clutch purse.

Geese patrol the space that is not-land,
not-pool. They creak, loud as old doors winched open.

She startles; circles her lips, pats her hand over the little hole
and lets go her ice-cream. It swims with ants.

He takes her picture. He will post it
like a card of *wish you were what you aren't*.

If these box trees weren't clipped so tight
they would grow anyhow they pleased.

Saint Catherine

It starts as a joke, the one about
the kitchen and what you're doing out of it. All smiles. Splay
of knees, bulge of crotches,

mutter of *heavens, these women.*
Why have a dog and bark for it? Keep your eyes open

for the tic of an index finger
shoving spectacles up a sweaty nose.

Keep running circles
round their gnawed faith. Jab and feint.
Jab and feint.

They will kill you
for being cleverer,
worse than laughing at their dicks.

You know all of that but
won't stop. Can't. You didn't read the Library of Alexandria
to bat your eyelashes and keep schtum.

This isn't about God,
the stained-glass legends of broken wheels, the barrowload
of miracles, or the dinner-plate halo they will nail to your head.

Under the gospel,
the truth of it: woman answers back, ends up dead.

The last pangolin

Taking a scale between thumb and forefinger, they peel the creature.
Leaf by brutal leaf, as one might strip an artichoke,
they tug it bare. Set their teeth to its sharp
and bitter edges, scrape off the smallest
lick of meat at the root. Only when
the final petal is torn away,
do they discover
there is no
choke, no
living thing,
no answer.

Extinction events

It fell before first flight. Nest to gutter in a dirty vertical,
a rook nestling stretches on the tarmac.

Skin pockmarked with the stubble of ungrown feathers,
still slippy with the lining of the shell's cracked fontanelle.

Eyes roll dull coins. Leg arrested in mid-step,
it scrapes with raptor claws,

as though the strata of the pavement split
and spread out a fossil dinosaur in miniature.

The stretched sack of its belly bulges
with the busy tenancy of maggots. Black, blue, magenta;

the entire paintbox of disgust. It cocks
a medusa head, wears its beak like the mask of a plague doctor.

~

It will be years before every part
of me is extinguished. A piecemeal dying-out.
It begins with the certain lock
of names to faces; nouns to things.

The flight of fancy grows clumsy, stutters.
Each small forgetting a chick elbowed
out of the mind's nest. That idea I had
five minutes past: going, gone. The space gawks.

I cling, frantic against the unfeathering
of the intellect; memory plucked to shivering gooseflesh.
Helpless as a hatchling, with the urge to fly
and only stumps with which to do it.

A flightless bird, I lurch through bare vocabulary.
Soon, this *corvus frugilegus* will be reduced
to *bird*, to *flying thing*, to *thing*, to lacuna.
Words without wings. I mimic Icarus:

quills slip their moorings, stream, as I claw
at tumbling air, plummet in a reverse evolution
from adult to juvenile, juvenile to nestling,
all the way back to egg. I squat inside the bland
shell of the skull, contents slippery.

The correct hanging of game birds

Rostrum
Select old, wild birds. Beware harsh beaks, horned spurs, claws toughened by years of defiance. Pierce the beak. Hang by the neck, the feet. Each man has his taste. Hook and hang them long enough to conquer disobedience.

Syrinx
Keep them in the dark. Convert the cellar into a hanging room: a stamped dirt floor to absorb the moisture they shrug off, dense walls to absorb sound. Keep your birds separate. Even when dead, their warmth communicates from breast to breast, stirs discord.

Pectoral girdle
Permit yourself the luxury of appreciation. This bird is yours, now. Dawdle on the ruffled collar, handsome as a rope of pearls around the throat; cheek blushed with pretty shadow; eye ringed with the purple-blue of bruising. Jewel plumage so thick it weighs down the wings. You can't imagine how she flapped or flew.

Breast
Pluck right away and you experience the thrill of naked flesh, but the body will dry out. Your bird is ruined. Wait three days, maybe seven. Then, and only then, strip off the feathers. Patience. Flesh and innards need time to ripen. Sublime flavour is attained when skin loosens its grasp on muscle. She oozes oil and perfume.

Rump

A gentle incision. Slice skin, not meat. Slide in up to the wrist and spread your fingers. Unpeel her body like wet fruit. Relish satin texture, the greenish shimmer of perfect ripeness. Keep going. Fillet scraps from bone, a job less bloody than you expect. Persistence rewarded with flesh that yields to your authority.

Lesser coverts

Lock the dog in the yard, to stop it lapping up the puddles that collect under the carcases. Ignore the neighbours complaining they can't sleep. The smile that shuts them up faster than any bellowed argument. The way they shrink away.

Cloaca

Time passes without needing to pay it much attention. Nights in the cellar, waiting for your birds. Their toes dripping, their eyes glazed. All resistance drained from them. The silence is balm, the scent delectable and rare. If only the dog would stop barking.

You can begin at almost any point

You are drinking enough to disappear. You, your body, everything you want to transform into nothing. All the women have gone. There are no bedclothes, no quilt, no arms to hug comfort. Find this bar again. A different bar. Sit. Drink. Add sugar. Bring aspirin. Bring me another beer. What do you have? Yes. Yes. Yes.

Wicker men

You wear the years like cages. Lashed tight with your toys, your wives, your kids, the faiths that make you hard and holy. You bellow how it's unfair, none of it's your fault. You'd show the whole damn world, if only someone would come and set you free. But there's no lock on the door. The gaps between the bars are big enough to squeeze through, always have been. The gasp and tickle of smoke. You sit, whining, waiting to catch fire.

They are an oddness

When he gets home, he slides you into a goldfish bowl.
You think there's no way you can fit, what with the tail
and fronds, but the water accommodates like a glove.

Morning and evening, he shakes a plastic tub. Food falls
in a drift of salty confetti. You flick your clever tongue
and catch each flake. You grow long and sleek.

He has to move you into the sink; by the end of the week,
the bath. He feeds you sardines from a tin. Holds out a fork,
says *here comes the aeroplane.*

When your lips close around the tines, you taste sweat
on his fingers. You eat, and grow. Your tentacles climb
the tiles around the tub. You pool the floor with slime.

At night, you rest your head upon his knee. He combs your hair
and whiskers, smoothes the creases from your frills
where they have wedged against the sides of the bath.

You wrap your tongue around him, squeeze till he gasps.
He gazes in wonder at the marks you leave,
his tongue small and lacking in muscle.

Phrenologist

Take my advice: develop a smaller skull.
It can be done, and though it's best to start
in childhood, even adults can force the mind
into submission. Strap wooden planks
to the sides of the head,
where bone is most open to persuasion.

Bind tight. Tighter. Squeeze out all that is undesirable:
ideas, intelligence, the daily effort
to put one word before the other.
There is little room for thought, but
consider the consolation: to float free
of that oppressive weight upon your shoulders.

Avoid dissent, any rapid shaking of the head.
A modest tilt of acquiescence
will stave off breakage. Treat yourself
as porcelain. You will chip easily.
But look at the pretty flowers around your rim,
The gilding, the pleasing ornament!

Eczema

Stretched to breaking point, she splits
                along the seams.
          Limbs littered with a dot-to-

dot that crusts knuckles, elbows,
                all the fractures of the body
          with scabbed lava. She is a fault

zone, trembling with forces that simmer
                beneath the surface.
          All day, she jails its heat. Slathers cream

to silence a furnace that tests each inch
                for weakness,
          poised to break out and brand her arms

with grafitti that betrays what's been forbidden
                to speak, to be.
          She itches to be a smooth girl with quiet skin

and expectations, slide through the world
                without snagging
          the corner of anyone's attention. But

the undesirable is leaking through; won't sit on its hands,
                keep its trap shut.
          She's wearing thin. Scared to read the angry scrawl;

that it'll tell her what she doesn't want to know
                and can't unwrite;
          that she's the same inside as out:

beastly, bloody, terrifying. At night, she surrenders.
Rakes herself raw.
What's inside sharpens its claws

and scratches back, mirror-writing that seems to spell
unpeel; escape
the pelt that binds her silent.

Planetary wobble

Earth refuses to draw clean circles. In a seven year itch,
she shimmies round the sun with an inbuilt deviation

from the true. What is truth? Not colouring inside the lines,
nor the fine print of little laws. Her fractal swing delights

in shapes swerving off-kilter, a rock-and-rolling calligraphy
of bad behaviour along the scroll of orbit. She sloshes oceans from neap

to spring; a dizzy, uncircled dervish swirl, close to God.
I am a whipped top that only spins a moment before

it topples from equilibrium; the gravity of doubt skews
my axis and I can't stand straight. Yet I will go on, tilted.

Long exposure

(Upway Wishing Well, Weymouth, 1904)

If asked, they'll say it's purely for the postcard photographer,
who arranged the scene: over there a chap with an unlit pipe,
a mother and daughter parked next to the well's mouth
and the pair of them, Miss Jansell and Miss Nellie Meek,
snarled up at the kissing gate. They embrace

for the long wind and snap of the shutter. Three minutes,
they hold the kiss. Tomorrow, they will go back,
Miss Jansell and Miss Nellie Meek,
and wish again, and kiss; without onlookers,
photographer, the clank and rattle of equipment.

They will keep wishing. Kissing through the years of hiding
in long grass, behind bushes, in closets, in plain sight.
Shoulder pressed to shoulder, pale-knuckled against all
that would put them asunder. Till everything
that twists fear into law unwinds.

When time comes to unknot concealment, shrug off
its whalebone cage. Till they can put an end to wishes;
stand up, brush off their skirts, and act.

The dark at the end of the tunnel

A woman walks upon the ocean floor.

Her skirt balloons around her legs

with the slow grace of a manta ray.

Her skin ripples, undulates.

Her stride is a keel, her chin a prow. She cleaves the thickness.

There was light.

There was a beach. Children, digging and screaming.

The filthy laughter of gulls, reek of bladderwrack.

There was a beginning: a paddle to the ankle mark. To calf. To knee.

There was the first gulp of brine.

The discovery of new ways to breathe.

Dappled sand she could sieve between her toes.

Reefs of jewel coral, sequin shoals of fish.

These are ghosts her hands swim through.

She's been walking underwater for so long that time moves to a
      different reckoning.

Her way is lit by the phosphorescence of angler fish.

Her companions are gulper eels that pause in their gnawing
      of whale carcases.

She no longer employs the agony of air in, air out.

Each footstep stirs grey clouds of ancient silk. Puffs of smoke to
      mark her passing,

towards a chasm where light loses all memory of itself.

Fox rising

Little hand that cuffs my wrist, under the table, where no-one can see. Little finger that lays its tongue along the inside of forearm, tip inching towards elbow crook, where blood beats. Sniff out the pulse. Tickle you under there.

Ah, my song of songs, my honeycomb, my bumble-bee, my pincushion, my red letter day. No harm can come when I hold tight. Let us play a game. Round and round the garden, like a –

Shh.
What made you say her name? Don't think of that shivery ripple, that shaking leaf, that split chestnut, that quaking mud puddle, that cracked window, that wishing well with eyes. Don't think.

Don't say her name or you'll call her. Do you want to be the one who's named, blamed for the whistle of her whine and how it blew down all our houses?

How can she rise, when foxes cannot climb? How, when the moon bites her tail each month and does not let her go? How, when she is stuck fast in night's bitumen fist?

What you mean to say is, hope is rising and with it, all our salvations. The fox is defeated. Chained in the pit two thousand years and two thousand more. The fox cannot rise, cannot disturb a dream, not by so much as a whimper.

Child, the lamps are bright. All is well. Nothing stirs the shadows beneath your bed, nor flickers at the foot of the stairs, nor hovers behind the door, breathing its hot breath when the lights go out.

I hear no whining, unless it be your own. I see no copper glint of eyes unless they be yours. I smell no fox-reek unless it be you. Are you fox? Do you want me to call fox on my own child?

Ah, my hinny, my coo, my ickle, my lickle, my lap and liquorice. There is nothing to fear. Nothing, my babby, my bonny, my bubble, my squeak. Mama could never be angry with her pickle, her pie, her cockle, her clam.

Now, here comes your supper to light you to bed. Open wide. Here comes the bear, the wolf, the tiger.

A child eats what it is told and when. Eat. You must. This is my body. Given for you. From the time when you were too young for an imagination. Eat.

Listen. I will show you the fox and then you will be afraid no longer. See, here she is. She is not your fox, but she is mine. There is more than one. Put your hand upon her, and believe.

Do mothers tell lies to their children?

Hush. There is no puss in this well, no jack in the green, no wolf at the door. Listen to me and not to the fears that come at 4am, the hour when those desirous of dying paddle away on an outbreath. Don't go with that crew. Stay with mama, between my breasts where the milk stands sticky in the nipples.

You are being very foolish. Do you want to see mama cry? Come. Hush your nonsense and take hold. Give me your paw.

I am stronger. She can pull all she likes. See, I can snap her in half with a flick of my fingers. I will never let you go. I am strong as a whirlpool, wide as an ocean and my tide will hold you safe in my harbour.

She cannot have you. No-one else can have you, not even yourself.

Quicksand

You wake from nightmare, throat glugging sludge.
She's already in the kitchen, arranging plates and cups.

It was an overnight stay, but that was a while ago.
A week? You search for the wall calendar.

Remember those Saturday morning TV serials? she purrs,
shuffling cutlery. *The hero always got stuck*

in quicksand. Flailing his arms.
Words scrolling across the screen. To Be Continued.

You're sure you never mentioned your nightmare.
You tilt a teaspoon towards the light. Your reflection flickers.

I dreamed of you last night, she says.
You press your lips together to stop

the question falling out. The kettle boils. Steam blurs
the window. The outside world disappears.

She arranges your favourite mug in front of you, and smiles.
Coffee, yes. You always feel better

after coffee. You lift the cup and flood your mouth
with a choke of liquid, dense with grounds.

Sleep of reason

For seven days I have not slept
more than an hour at a time; two on a good night.

I eavesdrop the fizzing lullaby
of the emergency lighting,

the shrieking wheels of the commode,
the machine that beeps my vitals every hour.

Night after wide-eyed night I'm defleshed
of the sine waves of dreaming that mark us human.

The nurse at the foot of my bed sighs,
flicks her pen along a line of boxes, strikes me from

her list of known mammals. De-classified, I drop off
the edge of this flat earth into a sleep of monsters

where dragons stretch their claws. I am no longer
mapped, safe. I lurch on insect legs, stripped

to an exoskeleton, the shrivelled thorax
of a wasp where my belly used to swell;

ribs tight as beetle wings, mouthparts clicking.
Dry hours whirr as I practice night vision

with composite eyes, smacking headlong over and over
into each hard bright morning, tough as plate glass.

Personal aphelion

I dawdle amongst absences. Men in white coats point out
crab constellations on the X-ray's sky, calculate the impact
of radiation; the glare of a sun that sears mass, flesh, optimism.

Bare-headed, I stumble round the ward, a lump of ash and ice
held together by movement. Blunder from misery too cold to calculate,
an occasional flirt with brightness, into an Oort cloud of unknowing.

At the end of hope's orbit, I uncentre childhood's
Ptolemaic cosmos with its selfish heart; shake off its myths
of immortality, inviolate faith. Trace the trajectory of sickness,

measure my continuance in millionths. Learn smallness,
how each cell makes new skin, new blood, new muscle. Discover
the curvature of space and time, a gravity strong enough

to haul my little cinder back. How each wound finds healing
in the opposite of itself, how something that is not finishing
bends itself into a return. Permit darkness, find light.

Dancing the plank

4am, ward-scuppered with all the other wrecks;
sick and storm-bowed by Cisplatin, salt in your veins.
Cling the rigging of the drip and hoist upright, sway
port to starboard. Build your sea legs.

So, you're dry-docked; mapped with poison
from wrist to elbow: blue anchors of old bruises,
red of heart tattoo. You are still Anne Bonney, Mary Read.
You've not sailed this far to scrape. Lean

into the swell of your rickety bed: peg-legged,
bilge-breathed, split-masted. Screw your eye
to the horizon and stagger
this day's plank. Kick up your heels.

Scar

Hesitation of flesh, you punctuate my forehead;
flick your apostrophe, your accent. Quote without
its unquote, you open and hang
                                        void.

                    Crack in the window
of the skull, you leak memory.

                    You are not
the tick of a teacher's pen that marks a piece of work
well done. Not *X* on the treasure map, a spit

on the dice and roll a lucky seven. Not
smart alec drumcrash punchline.

                    You are not
the end of the world.

                    You are
the narrow squeak,

thorn reminded of its crown,
swipe of lamb's blood on the lintel and the whistle of wings;

scrape of magpie claw as it roosts, scanning the treeline
for a mate to raise its stake from sorrow to joy.

Little glyph, scored on the brow's crease. My Braille
of stubborn bloody-mindedness. My dint.

Self-portrait as Halley's comet

I pick a spot so deep in the nothing
of the map it lacks a name;
fling the pebble of myself south

over the Tropic of Cancer.
Think I've hidden in a place too clever
to be unearthed; hope my black ice will shrivel in Sahara glare.

Like Halley, I go round and round
in patterns of freeze and burn; drag debris
I swear is negligible but leaves a filthy trail.

I chase my tail, learn nothing except
how to tear myself apart in tiny increments. Stuck in the rut
of orbit, I mistake flight for healing.

However many times I change
city, country, continent, I circle the same sun
unable to achieve escape velocity.

Perihelion is the closest a comet gets to the fire before managing to escape

1986 apparition was the least
favourable on record   *the worst*
          viewing for Earth observers
                    for the last 2,000 years

Khartoum, 1986. Pressed between man
and concrete balcony, I wait
for promised fireworks. To spark belief
this trapped feeling is flirtation,
I swig *arak*, the local firewater
that strafes the throat with gasoline.
I'm just a girl who can't believe she's here
until his attention sketches me from smoke
to solid. Alcohol mimics fullness,
but drains far too quickly through my punctures.

There.

He smears a finger across the sky, points at a blur
too dim for the name comet.

No.   There.

Halley. I thought we had a deal. You'd
stage a perfect flyby, a bells-and-whistles
shawl of flame across the sky, and I would
toe the narrow line of girl-wants-boy. But
you're playing peekaboo on the wrong
side of the sun, ripping up the book on
stellar etiquette and bending orbit to your
own kinked rules, while I'm trudging a
half-life in the mud of other people's
fairy tales. *One day my prince will,* etc.

I tip back another mouthful, gag, see stars of sorts. Out there,
Halley is trying to get the message through my signal crackle;
remind me how once upon a time
I splashed outside the lines;
didn't know it was
a mess, and didn't care. Before
I learned the science of satisfaction
was a man to fill my void with fitting colour.
Frightened of what life is like on other planets,
I hogtied to the safe trajectory of marriage, husband, happy ever.

orbital eccentricity

deviates   *from a perfect circle*   *irregular shape*

Halley orbits the sun in the   *opposite direction*

to the planets

Imaginary lines drawn in the sky.
No straight path through the universe;
not for Halley, not for me. Size of
a moon, and I couldn't see I was
kissing men to inoculate against
a gravity pulling in the opposite
direction. Running halfway round
the globe to achieve the impossible,
escape velocity from my queer core.

Late for his own perihelion, Halley skirts the thin breath of Mercury;
dodging asteroids, sprinkling meteors like kisses.
A bearded beauty teetering the tightrope,
he is all kinds of unruly. Has had
ten thousand revolutions to
imperfect his *bona to vada*
your dolly shriek up and
down the back alley
of the solar system,
and I have
just the
one.

       its dynamics cha otic

           and unpredictable on long   *timescales*

veering from orbit

Tonight or never.
On Halley's return I will be dust
that sifts the space between worlds.
Can keep shredding myself
with repetition
of what I don't want,
don't need; or accept
I'm erratic,
path spiced with deviation.

as Halley approaches the Sun, it expels
jets of sublimating gas from its surface
which knock it   off its orbital path
great enough
to significantly alter orbit

Man pours another shot, swirls the oily puddle. It reeks
of petrol. He leans in; laughs: *Baby can I light your fire?*
No to one more for *this* road. I am not locked into
the pull of a sun that will one day destroy me.
The sky is a blank page on which to sketch new charts;
off the map, a long way from a perfect   circle.

freed from the comet's icy core
jets of volatile material burst outward

the tail completely

breaks

off

Dark Matter

The night sky over Darfur overwhelms
with stars; so burdened, there are plans to cull
a quarter. A third. More. They will prune back
the constellations to chief brightnesses –
the named, the mapped – burn off the stubble
of the small, the feeble, the unclear.
Torch the unimportant to cinders.

They will dam the Milky Way, divert
its flow to those who appreciate fine light;
leave the star-field uncluttered
for Lords of the Empty Quarter:
Antares, Altair, Arcturus; extending
ashy vacancies between these oases
in the night's new desert.

Her name means Electricity

The wall of the student residence in Khartoum
is painted with a red and white sign. Nour pronounces it
Koo-Ka Koo-La, the blood and bone croak
of a bird of paradise shoving out its elbows.

I wonder why she coughs each time she calls me
until it clicks; it is a glottal stop,
an invisible letter lodged in the throat of her alphabet.

She asks the meaning of my name. I embellish:
star of the sea, flower of ocean, memory,
like the game of three statements: two truths, one lie.

Star-maps assure these night lights are the same as home.
Maia, Merope, Alcyone. I am overwhelmed by the magnitude
of light, names, distance between things that stand like sisters.

The correct digging of latrines

The schools are shut tomorrow: Sudanese Armed
Forces Day or some such. We hole up
in Mike's compound; it gets hairy
when the local lads start waving

their dad's farm tools, or Kalashnikovs.
They'll be back at their desks come Monday,
raising polite hands when I ask about past
participles. In the tight flicker

of the kerosene lamp we play
the drinking game: this week's most exciting
illness. Rupert wins with hepatitis.
My threadworms barely get a mention.

The roof beams tick with beetles. We get slaughtered
on wine made from sugar cane, debate
the bleary merits of long-drop versus
short-drop toilets, how fast we could dig

one, right now, tonight. Mike dabs his forehead
(malaria, runner-up) and says he doesn't give a shit
about hygiene; he's not staying
in this godforsaken hole a moment longer

than he has to. We fall about.
Rupert is the one to start it, grabbing
a spade. His eyes glow orange, like fires
seen at a distance. We're too pissed

to scoop more than a shallow trench.
Mike throws up and lies in it, groaning.
I can't stand for laughing. Flat out, watching
the stars swim, my intestines crawling with worms.

Goods to declare

At airport security, I set off alarms. Over the limit
with excess baggage; mistakes I packed into the past two years.

I upend the hourglass of my shoe, dust the red channel with Sahara.
Flip my passport to the photograph; it presses

its mouth to cellophane. Names, numbers blur
with the ink of time and distance. The guard pouts,

tries to put his finger on what has shifted. He swabs
my suitcase for ghosts as I rack my brains: the difficulty

of an answer to *did you pack this bag*
when I'm not the woman I was, not by a third. I am part-

smuggled; bloodstream a migrant community of cells
that have renewed, been replaced. Familiar, yet dislocated.

The customs officer seeks heat in my armpits,
between my thighs. He insinuates his fingers

through my clothing. The seams are sewn with desert.
I surrender their contraband; shake stars onto the sealed linoleum.

Biography of a comet in the body of a dog

All flap and gallop off the leash, it careers
in a wild orbit round the solar system. The sweep
of its tail makes skittles of doubt; it digs holes

through the wounded parts of joy
to the other side of despair. Every time
I toss hope away it brings it back, drops it

at my feet, tongue drooling a glittering rope.
On cinder nights when breath knocks hollow breath, it soars,
heart on fire, chasing squirrel stars it can never catch.

Auto-da-fé

Comets are not victims of their orbits.
The star round which they swing
neither rescuer nor persecutor. Their ring-a-rosie
is no procession of flagellants
lurching on bloodied knees towards the pyre.

I lay down the cat o' nine tails. Unlock
the scold's bridle, the girdle of barbed wire,
life as a succession of Ash Wednesdays.
Raise my forehead from dirt, learn fire
that is not immolation. Stand up. Dance.

Plunge

She pumps the sink, biceps clenched. Down there, the shunt
of chicken fat, a panicked nest of hair, the gristly glue of promises,
fag ends from when she gave them up, dinners scraped off the plate.

The hotel rooms they stayed in but never slept,
the corner she painted herself into, a mulch of bruises
from all those doors, bleach to make lies white again.

She ought to dump caustic soda down the hole; ought to
pickaxe the tiles masking rotten concrete, dismantle the whole system
and riddle the pipes with one of those steel snakes that rip muck to shreds.

Stargazer

Everywhere, there are bursts of radiance: faces that orbit
the bed at visiting hour; dwarf spots on the CAT scan, hot
as bullet holes. Sit down. Adjust to the vertigo tilt
of old words like spread, outlook, time. Doctors
murmur the names of new constellations
– *astrocyte, hippocampus, glioblastoma* – and calculate
the growth of nebulae; this rising tide of cells that climbs
the Milky Way of the spine to flood your head with light.

Now that you are not-you

and have satisfied the finger-check of pulse
at throat and wrist
ear to the chest
mirror to the lips

and you're done with the settle and sigh of blood
into the body's pockets
muscles relaxing in their last outstretch
the peaked hiccup of the red line becalmed

cells are climbing the spine's rope trick
up to where the brain is dizzy with electrons
like fireflies stoppered in a jar
and dying is the slow unscrewing of the lid

to release your dashing flutter of energies
as you unravel
shoot across the universe in lovely disorganisation
going
going
never gone

There is no there there

Universe encompassed on a blackboard. Arrowtip
of chalk traces perfect circle; path planted
with signposts (sun, planets, asteroids)
so that a comet cannot
lose its way, there
and back again.

I stay behind
to wipe away
powdered certainties.
Open the window, shake dust.
The comet shrugs off alphabets, textbooks, fingerposts,
pasts and futures. Eludes expectation. Continues, outwards.

The devil's in them

Past Slack Top, a cairn of bramble; leaves scorched
to charcoal by November gales. Berries clench
red fists, too late to ripen into black.

I jam my mouth with fruit; wedge teeth with seeds.
Pray for devilment to spark fire into this year of ash;
for rage to fly me off this ridge.

Foxes scream like teenagers spiked on gin.
A vixen breaks cover, skelters down the hill,
sets the flame of her tail to the bracken.

Bede writes a history of the English people

Ask, why I carve feathers to the spike of knives
when men are too busy to read. I should be bricking
windows into arrow-slots; should be bending
yew to longbows. The year roars with blood,
the murder of faith, and enemies close, closer.
Kings hammer mistrust into swords, demand
battle songs, and the world deafens with terror
of one's neighbour. I turn to words.
Their little lamps will outlive my flicker,
that of lords, and of this current fear. I grind
gall, vinegar, hone my quill. Feed the dark age with light.

And yet it moves

A comet does not live forever, although it measures its existence
in millions. With each orbit it shrinks, tattered by the journey
along the cinder track of space. A lantern burning its own flesh,
movement kindles destruction. All it can do is swing

around its star, streaming a distress flare; transfiguring
death of the self into incandescent beauty.
Even when too exhausted to glow, it tumbles over itself,
spitting debris. All things that move, live, and by extension, die.

I am burning up. Can't take my light to greater darkness,
so I spend it now, here. As I devour myself, I shall illuminate
my handful of turns around this little life, spread a glittering trail.

Since visiting the CERN Large Hadron Collider, you realise what you've been doing wrong with your life

In giant machines beneath the Alps, scientists
whack subatomic particles together; smash
protons round a loop of magnets to discover
something that can only be known by its absence.

You've spent a half-life as an experiment in forced collisions:
fists, spit, need. Walked into doors you should have slammed
behind you. Battered your heart in circles, hoping
next time it would turn out right. You didn't know

there were so many pieces a soul could break into,
how love can be conjured by sheer force of wanting.
All those shimmery nothings. Smaller and smaller specks of self.
Atom by atom, you rebuild. Begin to trust what's there, not

other people's shooting stars. The future expands
the faster you rush after, in a laughing game
of chase-me. You've nothing to prove. Leave
experiments in destruction to scientists.

Post mortem

Permit gentleness; there is worship here.
You were brought into this world with touch.
It is also your farewell.

Their hands make you beautiful.
They comb out the final tangles of hair;
mirror the curve of shoulder, elbow, chin;

ease soap along your limbs,
gentle as a mother bathes her child.
Such attention

to forgotten places of the body:
the pockets tucked behind the knees,
the small of the back, the armpits, cave of the ear.

As rowers push and pull the oar, their arms stiffen.
Regular and slow, they push and pull the cloth
in a lullaby of back and forth, writing love
into the parchment of your skin.

Let loose your moorings, the struggle to remain.
A short while, and their hands will not be necessary.
Till then, they edge you upstream,
away to where you are not.

How to keep breathing

When the world cannot be hurried or controlled,
there is the pleasure of laying on crisp bedlinen,
stretching it tight across the mattress, ready to receive.
The scent of a fresh-opened bag of coffee,
lemons preserved in salt, onions diced with a steel blade.

I can't stop thinking about jars.
The moment the lid is twisted off,
the contents begin to die.
If I had the sense, I'd stand at the counter
and spoon the whole lot down in one go.

Fullness answers some questions,
but not important ones.
I remember the taste of apricot kernel butter
bought in a Chinese supermarket thirty years ago,
and never found again. Like marzipan but better.

You are an X on the map, and more than that.
I ask you questions all the time.
Shoved to the brink of myself,
you give answers I can lean on.
Limbo is worse than bad news,

waiting for calls that don't come.
So we open every jar, every bag of coffee,
stick in our noses and haul breath into the lungs.
Chop onions to taste brine.
The bitterness of salted lemons.

When worlds collide

Four billion years from now, give or take,
the galaxy in which we're border-planted
will collide with Andromeda.

She is approaching
at a quarter of a million miles per hour,
sweeping across the heavens,
gathering universe in her wake.

She spreads spiral arms,
and we are arranging ourselves as strangers do
when good manners call for an embrace
but neither is sure how to hug.

As we fall towards each other,
we blink back interstellar grit
and wait for devastation
in an off the ten-to-the-power-of-zeros scale.

But each star will slide polite past star.
Solar systems will dance by the other
as water passes through water, rippling not ripping.

I should like to be there and witness the impossible:
every planet, asteroid, meteor, scrap of nebula dust,
the whole crash bang wallop shooting match
in a head-on collision, incandescent and gentle
and not so much as a scratch.

The autobiographies of stars

run to billions of pages, written in sentences spaced out
by the aeons it takes light to travel from one to the other.
Their chapters: loneliness, distance, the coda of supernova.

Peering upwards, I read texts pricked on indigo:
convoluted fairy tales of red giant, white dwarf, black hole;
the Perseids' flash fiction; nebula sagas of Horsehead, Crab, Orion –

they can only be read at night, when the world is half
darkness. I have to trust they're still out there
when daylight vanishes them in dazzle, and keep going,

keep putting one word after the other. Consider
the wink of my life: a tremble of gold leaf
clinging to vellum with the breath of the illuminator.

Bowing out

When she's exhausted all the places she can push food
around her plate, she shoves back her chair,
      – thick rug snagging its feet –

wads napkin to mouth, unwipes her smile,
and takes the first step backwards. Leaves the room.
      At the front door, she grabs the rope of her hair,

sweeps it above her head, combs it over nose and mouth.
Climbs the wrong way into her coat. Adjusts her arms
      to swivel in their sockets; buttons it back to front,

fingers clever at working out of sight. She unweds the gold ring
on her left hand; dismantles wristwatch,
      stops its ticking nudge.

Scrubs mud onto the soles of her shoes and quits the house.
Walking in reverse, she can't see what's coming.
      Knows if she can, she'll bottle out.

Her heels are discovering the way. On and on, further and further,
she leaves street, city, island, continental landmass.
      Unlocks gravity's shackle,

parts sky with shoulder blades and flees the planet.
The Earth shrinks to a speck she can eclipse with a fingertip.
      She unlocks the pearl keys of her vertebrae,

Shrugs off a deadweight of flesh. Shakes off breath's hard labour.
Keeps going, till there's no south or north, up or down.
      Planets unknot their orbits; the solar system undoes itself.

Here, where the universe is still breathing out,
she scatters into particles. Free of tracks facing in one direction:
      one exit, one entrance, one way through and out.

Notes

'Making Thunder Roar'. Commissioned by the Brontë Parsonage Museum for Emily200, celebrating the 200th Anniversary of Emily Brontë's birth.

'Palimpsest'. I'm adopted, and was 30 before I got my original birth certificate. It gives my birth name as Johanna Blight. If a couple were unmarried (as was the case with my birth parents), the father's name could only be included if he was present to sign the register.

'Eloping with a comet'. "Made it, Ma! Top of the world!" final lines of Cody (Jimmy Cagney), *White Heat,* 1949. "There are no battleships off the shoulder of Orion. No / C-Beams glittering off the Tannhäuser Gate." Inspired by the final lines of the replicant Batty (Rutger Hauer), *Blade Runner,* 1982.

'The correct hanging of game birds'. Latin terms refer to avian anatomy. Rostrum = beak, Syrinx = voicebox, etc.

'Personal aphelion'. Aphelion is the point in a comet's orbit where it is furthest from its star. Perihelion is the closest point.

'Perihelion is the closest a comet gets to the fire before managing to escape'. The most recent perihelion of Halley's comet was April 1986. It was the least impressive viewing from Earth for millennia. Halley's next flyby will be in July 2061. Sadly, that is also forecast to be a damp squib for Earth-based viewers.

Auto-da-fé. Auto-da-fé was the burning of a heretic by the Spanish Inquisition.

'And yet it moves'. 'Et pur si muove'. Words of Galileo Galilei (1564-1642), after being forced to recant (as in, 'recant or die') his discovery that the Earth moves around the sun, rather than the other way around.

Acknowledgements

Some of these poems have previously been published in:
Butcher's Dog, Confingo, Consilience, Dear Damsels, Extra Teeth, Freak Circus, Great Weather for Media, Loss Lit, New Welsh Reader, The North, Picaroon, Poem of the North, The Rialto, Riggwelter, Spelk, and *X-RAY Literary magazine.*

'Dark Matter' appears courtesy of Flapjack Press.

Poems have also won or been placed in the following competitions:
Bath Flash Fiction Award, The Casket of Fictional Delights, Hastings Writers Room 5/29, Hippocrates Poetry in Medicine Prize, Mslexia, Reflex & the Wigleaf Top 50. 'The topiary garden' was nominated for the Pushcart Prize 2018, and 'Extinction events' for The Forward Prize for Single Poem, 2018.

I am grateful to the Hawthornden Literary Retreat, where some of these poems were born.